II. Little Rock Ragtime

Martha Mier

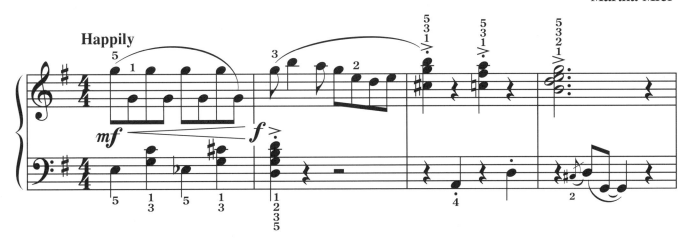

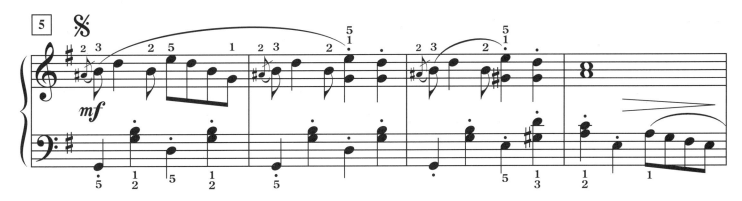

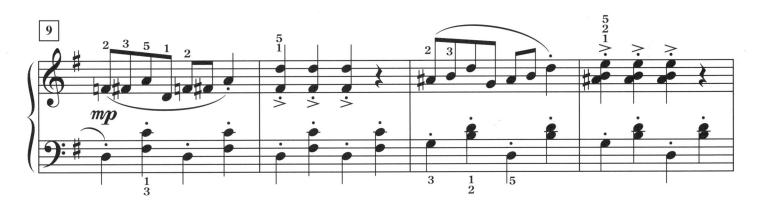

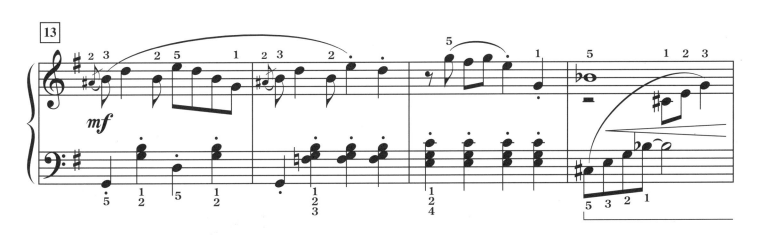

2nd time to Coda

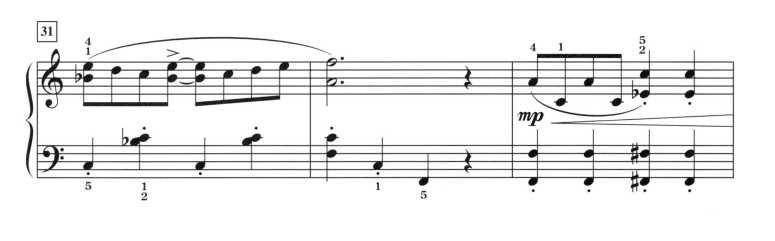

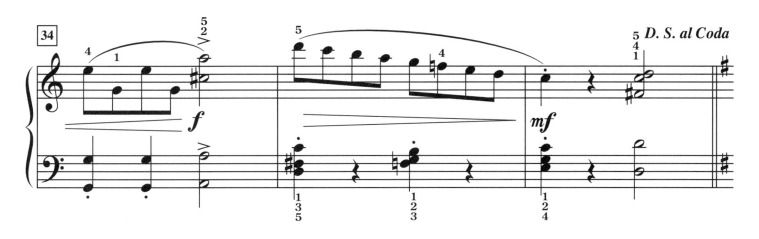

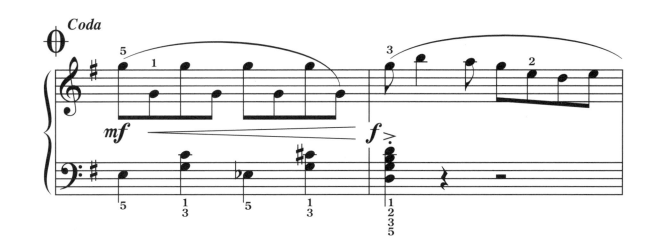

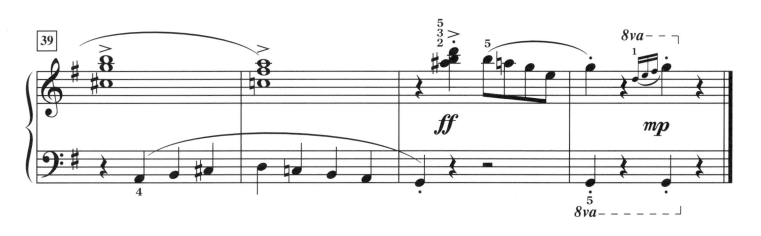

III. Red River Flows Gently

Martha Mier

IV. Finale
(Maumelle Celebration)

Martha Mier

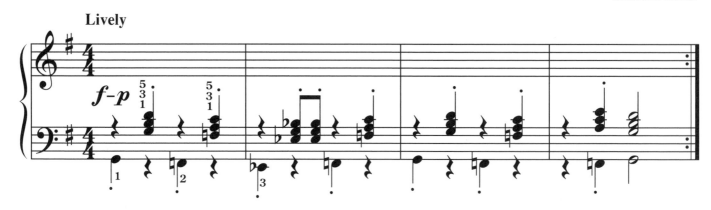

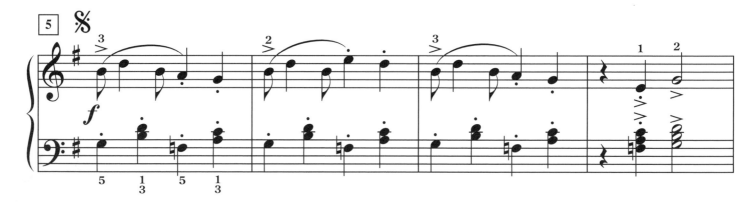

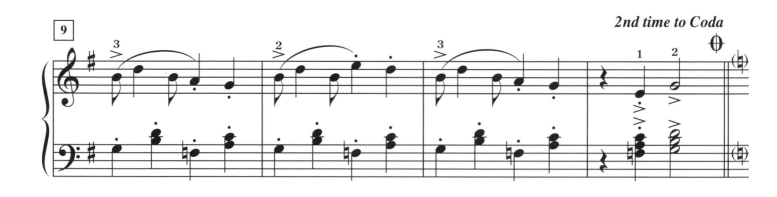

$3.50 in USA

Alfred's

RECITAL SUITE SERIES was created for performing piano

students. Each suite is a short collection of fresh-sounding solos carefully crafted to be played as a group in a recital. Musical challenges, appropriate for the level, provide interest and appeal. Aspiring pianists are challenged to reach higher degrees of excellence while playing music that is truly enjoyable for them and their audiences.

Martha Mier's
Arkansas Suite explores the sights and sounds of the state of Arkansas. It features four movements, each written in a different style. Students will travel to majestic Sugarloaf Mountain, experience a little ragtime in Little Rock, float gently down the Red River and celebrate in Maumelle through the music in this suite.

Intermediate (20781)

Tom Gerou's
California Coastline is a delightful snapshot of California seaside life. These three mildly contemporary solos are written in a variety of keys, yet technical challenges are comfortable due to carefully constructed melodic and rhythmic patterns. The music and the titles—*Carmel-by-the-Sea, A Golden Gate Afternoon* and *The Swallows of San Juan Capistrano*—represent three diverse California locations.

Late Intermediate (21321)

Gayle Kowalchyk's
New England Memories is a musical journey to the northeastern section of the United States. The changes of seasons so distinct in this region are represented in three romantic-style movements. *Autumn in Vermont* depicts the romance of the fall season—the joy of the beautiful foliage mixed with the sadness of the approaching winter. *Cape Cod Spring* is a quiet walk along the beach in the early morning—a memory of one of the first spring days. *Summers at Newport* brings to mind the fun of sailing along the coast in the summertime.

Intermediate (21322)

Alfred Publishing Co., Inc.
16320 Roscoe Blvd., Suite 100
P.O. Box 10003
Van Nuys, CA 91410-0003
www.alfred.com

ISBN 0-7390-2788-3

0 38081 19792 0